THE SUN & MOON SIGNS LIBRARY

LEO

23 JULY – 23 AUGUST

JULIA AND DEREK PARKER

Photography by Monique le Luhandre

Illustrations by Danuta Mayer

DORLING KINDERSLEY

London • New York • Stuttgart • Moscow

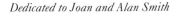

Dedicated to Joan and Alan Smith

A DORLING KINDERSLEY BOOK

Editor **Tom Fraser**
Art Editor **Ursula Dawson**
Managing Editor **Krystyna Mayer**
Managing Art Editor **Derek Coombes**
Production **Antony Heller**

Computer page make-up: Patrizio Semproni.
Photography: p 11 © Michael Holford/British Museum; p 16 Tim Ridley.
Stylist: pp 28-29 Lucy Elworthy. Illustration:
pp 60-61 Kuo Kang Chen. Jacket illustration: Peter Lawman.
With thanks to Carolyn Lancaster and John Filbey.

First published in Great Britain in 1992 by
Dorling Kindersley Limited, London WC2E 8PS

Visit us on the World Wide Web at
http://www.dk.com

A CIP catalogue record for this book is available
from the British Library

ISBN 0-86318-848-6

Reproduced by GRB Editrice, Verona, Italy
Printed and bound in Hong Kong by Imago

CONTENTS

INTRODUCING
LEO

LEO, THE SIGN OF THE LION AND KING OF BEASTS, IS THE
FIFTH SIGN OF THE ZODIAC. LEOS USUALLY MANAGE
TO ACQUIRE THEIR OWN INDIVIDUAL KINGDOMS OVER WHICH
THEY CAN RULE SUPREME.

The Zodiac lion or lioness rules skilfully, tactfully organizing others, and always expressing creativity in one form or another.

This sign is ruled by the Sun. In fact, it is almost as if the generous, bright, Leo personality derives from some inner sun. When such a force of personality fails to shine through, one can tell that something is seriously wrong. Leos who suppress their inner glow will be unhappy and unable to fully express their potential.

Traditional groupings

As you read through this book you will come across references to the elements and the qualities, and to positive and negative, or masculine and feminine signs.

The first of these groupings, that of the elements, comprises fire, earth, air, and water signs. The second, that of the qualities, divides the Zodiac into cardinal, fixed, and mutable signs. The final grouping is made up of positive and negative, or masculine and feminine signs. Each Zodiac sign is associated with a combination of components from these groupings, all of which contribute different characteristics to it.

Leo characteristics

Leo is of the fixed quality, which means that while Leos are generally stable people, they can also be very stubborn. They must, at all costs, curb any tendency towards being bossy or pompous, and limit their urge to overdramatize every problem.

As Leo is a masculine, positive sign, it inclines its subjects to be extrovert. Another characteristic that makes Leos easy to identify is their enthusiasm. This is, in fact, indicative of the sign's element: fire.

Most Leos prefer wearing the warm, opulent colours of the Sun, their ruling "planet".

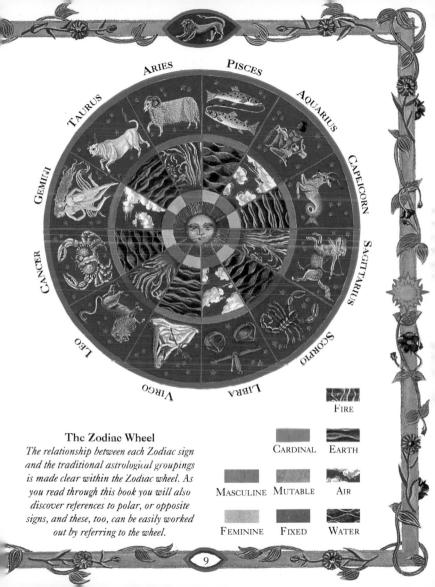

The Zodiac Wheel

The relationship between each Zodiac sign and the traditional astrological groupings is made clear within the Zodiac wheel. As you read through this book you will also discover references to polar, or opposite signs, and these, too, can be easily worked out by referring to the wheel.

CARDINAL

MASCULINE MUTABLE

FEMININE FIXED

FIRE

EARTH

AIR

WATER

MYTHS & LEGENDS

THE ZODIAC, WHICH IS SAID TO HAVE ORIGINATED IN BABYLON
AS LONG AS 2,500 YEARS AGO, IS A CIRCLE
OF CONSTELLATIONS THROUGH WHICH THE SUN MOVES
DURING THE COURSE OF A YEAR.

When one joins the major stars of the constellation Leo together, they do actually resemble a crouching beast. The Ancient Babylonians called the constellation the Great Dog. At least 5,000 years ago, the Egyptians gave it the name that is familiar to us today.

The Labours of Heracles

Like the Crab of Cancer, the Lion is associated with one of the 12 labours that the hero Heracles was made to perform by King Eurystheus, the ruler of Greece, as an atonement for slaughtering his own wife and children. After consulting the Oracle at Delphi, Heracles learned that only by showing obedience to King Eurystheus could he ever be forgiven for his dastardly crime.

Heracles's first labour involved killing and flaying an enormous lion, whose pelt was so tough that it could turn aside all weapons.

The Nemean lion

The lion, which lived at Nemea, in the Peloponnese, was born of Echidna the snake-woman and Typhon, a monster with a hundred eyes. The goddess Hera had sent it to inflict havoc upon the neighbourhood of Nemea, the plain of which was sacred to Zeus, king of the gods.

Meeting the lion on the slopes of Mount Tretus, Heracles first shot at it with arrows (it merely yawned as they rebounded from its skin), then attacked it with his sword, and finally struck it with his club. At this point, irritated by a headache, it bit off one of Heracles's fingers.

Heracles eventually resorted to the novel idea of choking the lion to death while it was resting in its cave. On trying to skin it, however, he found that its hide resisted all knives, so that he eventually had to use its own claws – the only instruments sharp enough. Heracles subsequently

Heracles and the Nemean Lion
*This Greek vase, which dates from 510 B.C., shows
Heracles struggling to overcome the seemingly
invincible Nemean lion.*

wore the lion's impenetrable skin as armour, with the head as a helmet. The lion itself was set in effigy among the stars by Zeus.

Leo characteristics

It is, of course, virtually impossible to determine how various human qualities became associated with a particular sign of the Zodiac. It can, however, be said that those born with the Sun in Leo are extremely likely to possess the unmistakably proud demeanour of lions, and that they seem to be just as invulnerable to attack. Indeed, bravery, strong leadership, and forcefulness of personality are all definite Leo characteristics. However, when Leos are troubled, they will retire to some private place in order to recover from their wounds in solitude.

SYMBOLISM

CERTAIN HERBS, SPICES, FLOWERS, TREES, GEMS, METALS, AND
ANIMALS HAVE LONG BEEN ASSOCIATED WITH PARTICULAR
ZODIAC SIGNS. SOME ASSOCIATIONS ARE SIMPLY FUN, WHILE
OTHERS CAN BE USEFUL, FOR INSTANCE IN MEDICINE.

Flowers

*The sunflower, marigold, and
celandine, all of which reflect the
vibrant colours of this sign, are
ruled by Leo.*

MARIGOLDS

SUNFLOWERS

Herbs

All herbs are believed to be ruled by Leo. This is particularly true of angelica, which "comforts the heart", eyebright, which is good for all eye ailments, and pimpernel, which alleviates toothache.

BAY

ANGELICA

Trees

The bay, palm, and walnut are traditionally Leo trees. The same is true for the orange, lemon, and all other citrus trees.

ARECA PALM

Spices

No spices are specifically connected with Leo. As a fire sign, however, Leo must surely rule pepper and mustard.

MUSTARD

PEPPER

LEO
SYMBOLISM

BRASS LION'S HEAD DOOR KNOCKER

Animals
The lion is, naturally, the Leo animal, but all other big cats are also ruled by this sign.

DIAMANTÉ TIGER BROOCH

Metal
Gold is the Leo metal, not only because of its association with the Sun, but also because of Leo's unquestionable taste for riches.

WOODEN TIGER FOLK CARVING

GOLD

LEOPARD CIGARETTE LIGHTER

RUBY EARRINGS

RUBY BROOCH

RUBY NECKLACE

TOY TIN LION

Gem
The dark red, glowing ruby, the colour of the Sun at dusk, is ruled by this sign.

LEO
PROFILE

THE LION'S MANE OF HAIR, THE UPRIGHT STANCE, AND A RATHER
CONVENTIONAL, BUT VERY DASHING IMAGE, CHARACTERIZE
THIS DRAMATIC ZODIAC SIGN. LEOS MAY SOMETIMES CONVEY AN
IMAGE OF HAUGHTINESS TO OTHERS.

M ost Leos stand well, with their feet placed slightly apart and their legs held straight. They make strong, meaningful gestures which are carried through in a distinctive and often dramatic way.

The Leo face
You are likely to have a noble face, with bright, clear eyes.

The body
Generally speaking, the Leo spine and back are erect, which gives people of this sign the appearance of height even if they are not tall. Leos are typically broad shouldered, and most have admirably slim waists. This can be a decided asset when fashion decrees an emphasis on that area. Leos usually move well, and should aim to keep their elegant, cat-like agility well into old age. Your feet and hands are unlikely to be large, and you will probably be small boned in comparison to members of most other Zodiac groups.

The face
You will tend to hold your head high. If you decide to leave your hair to grow long it will probably become as luxuriant and flowing as a lion's mane, although it may sometimes be equally untameable. Most Leos have clear complexions, and are likely to tan well. There is often a striking nobility about the Leo forehead and face that you may well possess. If you are a typical Leo, your eyes are likely to be very bright and clear, with perhaps slightly drooping eyelids, and your nose may be large

The Leo stance
In keeping with their outgoing manner, Leos stand well, and are prone to making bold, meaningful gestures.

and prominent. Some Leos develop an unfortunate habit of looking down their noses at other people, considering them to be inferior. However, you will not find it hard to break into a wide, sunny smile.

Style
Of all the Sun signs, Leo probably has the best sense of style. Since most Leos enjoy making a dramatic impact, there is often something eye-catching or spectacular about the things that they decide to wear.

Designer jeans and designer labels are very popular among Leos. However, people of this sign should make sure that they control their showiness, since too much glitter can ruin their image. Similarly, although Leos are generally inclined to buy high-quality, slightly conservative clothes, many of them will rashly spend enormous sums of money on dazzling but terribly impractical outfits which they can only wear once. Most Leos learn with experience. People of your Sun sign usually look marvellous in the colours of the Sun,

from palest lemon and pink to darkest orange, with younger people liking the brightest colours.

In general
Because the Leo body reflects the Leo psychology, it is not difficult to tell how happy a Leo is. If Leos are upright and smiling, then their psychological Sun, which is a part of every Leo, is shining, and all is well.

PERSONALITY

GENEROSITY AND ENTHUSIASM ARE BOTH DOMINANT LEO
TRAITS. WHILE LEOS ENJOY TAKING CENTRE STAGE,
THEY WILL ALSO ENCOURAGE THEIR LOVED ONES AND
FRIENDS TO GET THE MOST OUT OF LIFE.

Being positive and enthusiastic in outlook, Leos have a great zest for life and, if only because they put so much into it in the first place, they will get a great deal out of it. Every day has to be lived to the full, and inner satisfaction comes when you settle down to relax at the end of the day and realize that not only has each of your tasks been well and truly completed, but also that there is something to show for all your efforts.

At work

As a Sun sign Leo, your organizational ability is almost certain to be excellent. You can, however, sometimes express your love for organization in an extremely bossy way. This tendency towards becoming too dominant over people must be controlled, if it is not to be a source of embarrassment to your family and friends. Should you find yourself in charge of a situation (as

Leos so often are), you should ensure that you hand out instructions with as much charm and warmth as you can. Bear in mind that other people thrive on receiving encouragement and praise, just as you do.

Your attitudes

Leos are known to hate pettiness of any kind. You will be very good at comprehending the overall plan and concept of a project, but will then willingly leave the smaller, fussy details to other people. Small-minded behaviour and nit-picking arguments will no doubt infuriate you. When you encounter these, what might very accurately be called your "lion's roar" will be heard, and you will put the culprits thoroughly in their place.

Leos usually have a well-developed sense of drama, which definitely needs to be tempered with a little restraint. At its best, however, it will provide you with a great sense

The Sun rules Leo

Apollo, the Greek Sun god, represents the Sun that rules over Leo. The Sun inclines its subjects to be generous, affectionate, and creative.

of occasion. You will have no trouble making something special out of every get-together that you are party to, and will love to entertain people extravagantly.

The overall picture

Firmness, determination, and decisiveness are marvellous qualities. Dogmatism and stubbornness are, however, quite the opposite. It is in this area that you must tread very carefully. Although it can be quite difficult for you to develop an ability to be flexible, it will help if you consciously remember that the best rulers are those who are understanding, reasonable, and fair – especially when pronouncing judgement on other people.

LEO
ASPIRATIONS

Flair, enthusiasm, and showmanship must find a place in any Leo career. Make sure that you are able to use your excellent organizational ability, whatever your career aspirations are.

Fashion and jewellery design
Leo is the most creative of all the signs. You may love high fashion, and could design and make your own jewellery.

WATERCOLOUR
PAINTS

DESIGNER EARRINGS
AND BROOCH

Teaching
As they are so creative, Leos often make fine teachers of the arts. Their natural enthusiasm inspires their students.

ARTIST'S PALETTE

SABLE PAINTBRUSHES

VENETIAN
FESTIVAL
MASK

The theatre

*A career in the theatre, which would
combine a number of the qualities
traditionally associated with
Leo, may strongly
appeal to you.*

1912 FOOTBALL MEDAL
AND REFEREE'S WHISTLE

Professional sport

*Leos find sport and
exercise important, and like to take a pride in
their bodies. You could therefore find the idea
of a career in professional sport attractive.*

LEAD MODEL SOLDIERS

The armed forces

*Leos have great powers of leadership. You
may do well in the armed services, and
could rise to a position of authority.*

Illustration

*Leos often turn their artistic
talents to illustrative
drawing or painting.*

CHARCOAL

Health

MORE THAN ANY OTHER ZODIAC TYPE, LEO NEEDS TO BE FIT IN
BOTH MIND AND BODY, WHICH ARE UNIQUELY CONNECTED
IN THIS SIGN. AN INJURED BACK CAN, FOR INSTANCE PROVOKE
DEPRESSION, AND A PRESSING PROBLEM, A HEADACHE.

The lions of the Zodiac will rapidly fall into black moods if some injury threatens to cramp their action-packed lifestyles. You will become very bad-tempered with yourself if such an injury forces you to stay away from your health club; and your irritation with an injury may far outweigh your pain or discomfort. This is because you really do not like wasting time, or neglecting something you love doing. Fortunately for you, and perhaps for those who know you, this kind of situation does not arise all that frequently.

Your diet

Mineral salts are considered to be a necessary part of the human diet. Because of modern eating habits, however, our supply of them is often unbalanced. You may benefit from supplementing your diet with the cell salt Magnesium Phosphate (Mag. Phos.). This is good for the heart, and aids relaxation. You should also make sure that you control the amount of cholesterol you consume.

Taking care

The Leo body area is the spine and back. Backrest chairs are an excellent idea, as is exercise geared to strengthening the back; these will help you to avoid backache, which is often just a sign of stress. The Leo organ, the heart, also needs to be exercised, if it is to be kept in as good a shape as other organs of the body.

Leos are usually strong and healthy, with mind and body at one with each other. You must be careful that you do not outstrip your energy and end up being forced to take a rest. Keeping a balance is therefore important for you. Of course, do not lose sight of the fact that when you do set aside time to relax, you will enjoy it with full Leo panache and luxury-loving extravagance.

Astrology and the body

For many centuries it was impossible to practice medicine without a knowledge of astrology. In European universities, medical training included information on how planetary positions would affect the administration of medicines, the bleeding of patients, and the right time to pick herbs and make potions. Each Zodiac sign rules a particular part of the body, and early medical textbooks always included a drawing that illustrated the point.

LEO AT LEISURE

EACH OF THE SUN SIGNS TRADITIONALLY SUGGESTS SPARE-TIME
ACTIVITIES, HOBBIES, AND HOLIDAY DESTINATIONS.
ALTHOUGH THESE ARE ONLY SUGGESTIONS, THEY OFTEN WORK
OUT WELL, AND ARE WORTH TESTING.

Astrology
*Due to their eagerness to help other
people make the most of their
potential, Leos often make
enthusiastic astrologers.*

TOOLS FOR ASTROLOGICAL
CALCULATIONS

Amateur theatre
*Leos generally enjoy amateur
theatre. It gives them an
opportunity to express their
natural dramatic flair, and
allows them to show off a little.*

GREASEPAINTS

POSTAGE STAMPS

Travel

*Comfort, or even luxury, should be the
hallmark of your holiday. You would
rather spend a day in a five-star hotel
than a month in a tent. Italy, Iraq,
the South of France, and the Alps
all appeal to Leo.*

The Sun

*Leos love enjoying the Sun. Its
light and warmth give them a sense
of well-being, making them feel
positive and optimistic.*

NAPKIN
AND CUTLERY

Eating out

*You no doubt have a great
sense of style and occasion,
and therefore only the best will
be good enough for you when
you choose to eat out.*

LEO IN
LOVE

WHEN LEO FALLS IN LOVE, THE WORLD TAKES ON A GOLDEN
GLOW – BUT WHEN LEO IS REJECTED OR UNLUCKY IN
LOVE, THE STORM CLOUDS GATHER AND WOUND-LICKING
TAKES PLACE, IN THE PRIVACY OF THE LAIR.

The majority of Leos put their partners on pedestals. You may be the king or queen of the Zodiac, but you will also enjoy playing consort to your partners. This means that when things go wrong, you can suffer more than most Zodiac types. Disillusion and heartbreak are common, and are sometimes followed by a loss of self-confidence that only time can heal. Unfortunately, some Leos are less psychologically developed than others, and will tend to dominate a weak partner. At times this may prove successful, if that partner is the type of person who needs a great deal of support; but both parties must aim to achieve a happily balanced relationship based upon sharing.

The generosity attributed to Leo will certainly be expressed when you are in love. The wrong partner may feel that you are showing off, or trying to impress. This is not so, since with you "celebration" is the keyword, and to blazes with the cost.

As a lover
The fire element of Leo burns strongly and brightly when you realize that you are in love. You will want your partner to share the sheer joy and exuberance of your

positive expression of emotion, through psychological rapport and friendship, as well as through rewarding and fulfilling sex. It is equally important for all Leos to have partners who are able to share an enthusiasm for their interests.

expression of love: when in love, life for them becomes one huge, romantic musical, opera, or film. Some other Leos display, very surprisingly, a certain modesty. Finally, there are those Leos who are never really psychologically whole until they are sharing their life with a partner. Premature commitment is a danger for these types.

Types of Leo lover

Many Leos are flirtatious, enjoying friendship as well as love and romance with their lovers. They need partners who are their intellectual equals. Other Sun sign Leos are very sentimental. They may tend to create a claustrophobic atmosphere within a relationship and, should a partner decide to break away, will find it difficult to accept the fact that the romance has ended. Many Leos are totally leonine in their

LEO AT
HOME

A LEO'S WARM AND WELL-LIT HOME WILL REFLECT THE HIGHEST
STANDARDS OF COMFORT. ELEGANCE, STYLE, AND BEAUTY
ARE THE KEYNOTES AND, EVEN ON SLENDER MEANS, THEY WILL
USUALLY BE ACHIEVED.

Wherever Leos end up living, they always strive to make their homes very special places. You will probably spend a great deal of money on beautiful things, and on improving your home, for precisely this reason. Your home is likely to be luxurious, colourful, and warm. If you have a garden, you have probably filled it with many different types of colourful flowers, and if the climate permits, you may grow attractive exotic fruits and vegetables.

Classical sculpture
Leos often own a copy of an ancient sculpture.

beautiful surroundings that are stylish, luxurious, and easy on the eye. You take great pride in your home, and will, as has already been said, spend a lot of money on it, making sure that the furniture and decor you choose is unlikely to become boring after a year or two. In this way you will avoid the disruption of the constant necessity for change. Quality is likely to be very important to you, and Leos sometimes have a marked tendency towards showiness that should be controlled. You may, for instance, manage to overdo a room by placing too much elaborate and obviously expensive furniture together, and perhaps in quite inappropriate places.

Furniture
When it comes to choosing furniture for your home, your decisions are probably based around elegance and comfort. Leos like to relax in

Exotic wallpaper
Leo furnishings are often striking, like this wallpaper in the style of William Morris.

Soft furnishings

Texture and warm, glowing colour are both important: many Leos favour rich silks and brocades, or velvet which will deepen and enhance the colours that they choose. Although you may be very much attracted to fur rugs, Leos are among the leaders in the conservation of wildlife, and are especially sympathetic towards the big cats. No self-respecting Leo would decide to own a real lion- or tiger-skin rug; it will have to be a high-quality imitation.

Decorative objects

Only the best is good enough for Leos, whatever decorative objects they may choose. Therefore one finds ornaments in the Leo home that are as near to perfection as can be afforded, and some that may have strained the individual's purse-strings.

Your glass will be the finest crystal, and the paintings, which you may have produced yourself, will be beautifully framed. Leos like classical things, so a museum reproduction of a fine Greek sculpture or a copy of a Roman emperor sitting on his horse may also make an appearance.

Colourful armchair and cushion
The golden colours of this chair and cushion reflect the colours of the Sun, which are so dear to Leos.

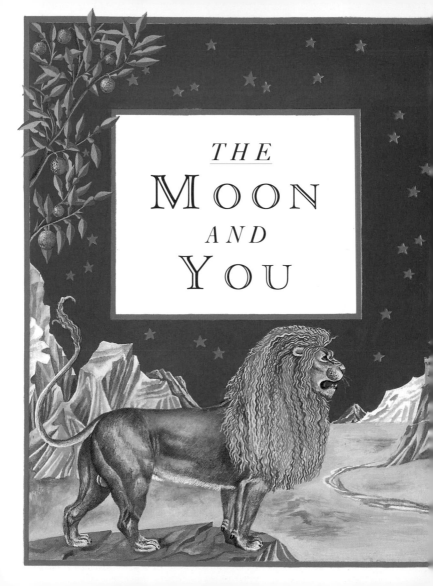

THE
MOON
AND
YOU

THE SUN DECREES YOUR OUTWARD
EXPRESSION, YOUR IMAGE, AND MANY
IMPORTANT PERSONALITY TRAITS. THE
MOON, ALTHOUGH MERELY THE EARTH'S
SATELLITE, IS ASTRONOMICALLY THE
SECOND MOST IMPORTANT BODY IN THE
SOLAR SYSTEM. FROM THE SIGN THAT IT
WAS IN AT YOUR BIRTH, IT INFLUENCES HOW
YOU REACT AND RESPOND TO SITUATIONS,
YOUR EMOTIONAL LEVEL, AND, TO A CERTAIN
EXTENT, WHAT YOU HAVE INHERITED FROM
YOUR PARENTS AND ANCESTORS. HAVING
FOUND YOUR MOON SIGN IN THE SIMPLE
TABLES ON PAGES 56 TO 59, TURN TO THE
RELEVANT PAGES AND TAKE A STEP
FORWARD IN YOUR OWN SELF-KNOWLEDGE.

THE MOON IN
ARIES

A COMBINATION OF TWO FIRE SIGNS GIVES YOU A HIGH LEVEL OF
PHYSICAL AND EMOTIONAL ENERGY, BUT YOU MUST LEARN
TO CURB HASTINESS AND SELFISH REACTIONS TO PARTNERS. YOU
ARE MORE CASUAL THAN MOST LEOS.

Basically, you are a very energetic person with a powerful motivation to win, and your Leo organizational ability will enable you to take over any critical situation at the drop of a hat.

Self-expression

You will, unfortunately, express Leo bossiness from time to time. But the lively, positive influence of your Arien Moon makes it unlikely that you will put other people's backs up too much. Your Arien Moon will also mitigate any Leo pomposity.

You should avoid being too hasty, since this could lead you into premature and ill-considered action. Learn from your past mistakes and pace yourself. You may not be too good at coping with detail; perhaps you need the help of others once you have mapped out an overall plan. You have formidable resources of energy, and could easily have a flaring temper.

However, neither Aries nor Leo harbours resentment, and Leo magnanimity usually emerges soon after any explosion of anger.

Romance

Your Arien Moon makes you a very passionate and lively lover, and your natural *joie de vivre* is both infectious and attractive. The worst Arien fault is selfishness: at times, you may react selfishly, which is not very endearing.

You are among the most highly sexed of Leos, and will probably fall in love at first sight. You will expect an equally positive and immediate response from prospective partners. Remember that not everyone is immediately as sure of their feelings as you, and try to develop patience.

Your well-being

The Arien body area is the head, and you may suffer from an above-average number of headaches. Often, these

The Moon in Aries

will be caused by other people. Arien headaches may also sometimes be caused by slight kidney disorders.

You are probably somewhat accident-prone, through hastiness and your quick reactions. Take care in tricky circumstances.

Planning ahead

Your Arien Moon can make you somewhat impulsive financially, and you may tend to put too many eggs in one basket, if you are convinced that an investment will be lucrative. A little caution is advisable, since over-enthusiasm could be your downfall.

Parenthood

You will be among the most enthusiastic and encouraging of parents, making time to enjoy your children, and seeing to it that their out-of-school life is full of activity. Learn to enthuse about their projects, and you will have fun. You should have no generation gap problems.

THE MOON IN
TAURUS

LEO LIKES THE BEST AND MOST EXPENSIVE OF EVERYTHING. YOUR
TAUREAN MOON IS IN SYMPATHY. SINCE YOU NEED
MONEY FOR ALL THOSE LUXURIES, TRY TO DEVELOP YOUR BUSINESS
SENSE. MAKE AN EFFORT NOT TO BE FLASHY.

You are lucky, since in astrology the Moon is said to be "well placed" in Taurus. This means that it will exert a strong influence upon you. Your Moon sign will make you very reliable and dependable.

Self-expression
You need an above-average sense of emotional and financial security; if you achieve both you will flourish.

Your Leo liking for luxury and quality will certainly be enhanced by your Taurean Moon since, after Leo, Taurus is the sign of the Zodiac most inclined towards such pleasurable things. Your Taurean Moon makes you practical and down-to-earth, and you will work hard and persistently to achieve your objectives.

Romance
Your Leo passion is enhanced by Taurean sensuality, and you are usually faithful. But you must remain

aware that the worst Taurean fault, possessiveness, can very easily overcome you. Try to counter this negative trait with Leo magnanimity.

Your well-being
The Taurean body area is the throat. If your particular love is singing, you will really have to cosset it, since colds will at once settle in that area.

Very often, Taureans have a fairly slow metabolism. To prevent excessive weight gain, make sure that you exercise regularly. It is important to remember, too, that Taurus may have given you a sweet tooth, so control your intake of heavy, rich cakes and chocolates.

Planning ahead
Your luxury-loving instincts will decree that you need to earn rather a lot of money. Fortunately, your Moon sign endows you with a very good financial instinct, and you should

The Moon in Taurus

follow it. You will probably know intuitively when to invest and what to invest in, and will not over-extend yourself in any one area.

A credit balance on your bank statement will give you much satisfaction (and proof of hard work well done); you will also be keen to make your money work for you.

Parenthood

You will make a good parent, and will not allow your children to waste time. Both Leo and Taurus are disciplined signs, so you will be fairly strict with your children – at times, you may even be a little hard on them. Your children will certainly know where they stand with you: what you say is exactly what you mean. There will be no nonsense. But think carefully about this; sometimes you might just be too inflexible. Try to keep abreast of your children's opinions, and make sure that you move with the times. Otherwise, in spite of an excellent set of values, you may encounter generation gap problems.

THE MOON IN
GEMINI

YOUR LEO CREATIVITY COULD BLEND WITH YOUR GEMINIAN GIFT
FOR COMMUNICATION AND MAKE YOU A WRITER. DO NOT
OVER-RATIONALIZE YOUR EMOTIONS, OR TALK SO MUCH THAT
THERE IS NO TIME FOR ACTION.

The fire of your Leo Sun is fanned and encouraged by your air sign Geminian Moon, which makes you respond to situations in a powerful, rational, and intellectual way. You are very quick-witted, and always ready with some pertinent and original remark. The Leo tendencies to formality and pomposity are unlikely to emerge in your personality.

Self-expression
You are extremely versatile, and may tend to flit rather too readily from one interest or project to the next. Try to avoid superficiality, and falling into the trap of leaving a clutter of unfinished tasks and abandoned hobbies in your trail.

Your Leo creativity could find expression through writing, or perhaps in some glamorous craftwork – using, for instance, precious or semiprecious stones, crystals, metals, or fabrics. You do not lack enthusiasm, but may have

to make a conscious effort to keep it on the boil, since boredom and that peculiarly Geminian fault, restlessness, could overtake you.

Romance
You may question or rationalize your emotions, especially when you first realize that they are moved. Make quite sure that you do not suppress your emotions altogether, as your whole personality will suffer if you do.

In love, you can be both lighthearted and passionate. When friendship embraces full, physical love all the notes of your Leo personality will be sounded.

Your well-being
The Geminian body area covers the hands and arms, which may be particularly vulnerable to accidents. The Geminian organ is the lungs. It is absolutely vital that anyone with a Gemini emphasis who is a smoker

The Moon in Gemini

should try to limit or stop the habit.
Consult your doctor right away if a
cough settles on your lungs.

Planning ahead

Leos love quality goods, and need to
earn as much money as possible. You
may be attracted to well-sounding
moneymaking schemes with speedy
and generous returns on capital. Be
cautious: you could lose more than
you gain. Take professional advice in
these matters. Because you are among
the most versatile of Leos, you may

want to organize your life in a way
which ensures that you have two
different sources of income. You
could, for instance, take a hobby to
professional standards and then go on
to market it in some way.

Parenthood

You will be among the liveliest of Leo
parents, Gemini having the reputation
of being the most youthful sign of the
Zodiac. You will be young at heart
(and probably body), and your
children will appreciate the fact.

THE MOON IN CANCER

THE SUN AND MOON ARE IN THE SIGNS THAT THEY RULE, AND YOU
THEREFORE HAVE A PERFECT BLEND OF POSITIVE AND
NEGATIVE ELEMENTS. USE YOUR LEO SELF-EXPRESSION, AND
FOLLOW YOUR CANCERIAN INTUITION AND INSTINCTS.

The Sun and Moon, the two most powerful bodies in the Solar System, work very strongly and well for you; their influences combine to give you some excellent personality traits that you should always aim to use to your full advantage.

Self-expression

Your Cancerian Moon adds a very potent intuition to your Leo Sun sign characteristics, and powerful instincts that you should nurture: if you instinctively feel that you should take a certain line of action, then go ahead and do so. Your Moon sign also gives you a very powerful and vivid imagination that should be expressed creatively in some way.

By harnessing this quality, you may well produce some great work in arts and crafts. Take care that you do not let your imagination get out of hand, since you may have a tendency to worry unnecessarily.

Romance

Your emotions are highly charged: the fiery, assertive, and enthusiastic emotion of Leo is joined by the more tender, sensitive emotion of the Moon in Cancer. You will not find it difficult to express your feelings to your loved ones, be they lovers, children, or a household pet. Your protective instinct is also very strong and, while you are a wonderfully exuberant and passionate lover, you may at times tend to mother your partners. Be careful, as you may create a rather claustrophobic atmosphere within your relationships.

Your well-being

You are far more prone to worry than most Leos. To counter any unnecessary anxiety, allow your Leo optimism plenty of free expression.

The Cancerian body area covers the chest and breasts. Women with this emphasis should examine their

The Moon in Cancer

breasts regularly – although it is important to realize that it is mere coincidence that the name of the sign is the same as that of the disease.

Planning ahead
Your Cancerian Moon gives you a clever and instinctive business sense. You are able to invest wisely and shrewdly, although you could feel a certain amount of conflict in this area. The Leo you is very generous and enjoys spending money on pleasure and beautiful things, while your Cancerian instinct tends to make you more careful with money. A fascinating and very lucrative hobby for you could be to start an unusual collection of some kind, of objects that will increase in value over the years. This will make positive use of your Cancerian hoarding instinct.

Parenthood
You will be a very canny and enthusiastic parent, and will encourage your children to express their own potential as fully as possible. Try not to be overly protective towards them, and allow them to leave the nest and make their own lives when they feel the need.

THE MOON IN
LEO

BECAUSE BOTH THE SUN AND THE MOON WERE IN LEO ON THE
DAY OF YOUR BIRTH, YOU WERE BORN UNDER A NEW
MOON. LEO IS A FIRE SIGN, AND THIS ELEMENT POWERFULLY
INFLUENCES YOUR PERSONALITY AND REACTIONS.

S hould you study a list of the characteristics of your enthusiastic, optimistic, and positive Sun sign, you will realize that a great many apply to you. On average, out of a list of, say, 20 Sun sign characteristics, most people will identify with 11 or 12. For you the average increases considerably, because the Sun and Moon were both in Leo when you were born.

Self-expression
Your Sun sign makes you very positive in outlook and gives you exceptional organizational ability, plus a great deal of creative potential. Your Moon adds a powerful urge to express these qualities fully. Bear in mind that as there is an additional emphasis on the fixed quality of Leo, you may sometimes be inflexible.

You will react to most situations in a very Leo way, expressing the ability to take over at a moment's notice –

especially in a crisis. You can also be extremely bossy and dogmatic. Take note if you are accused of these unattractive characteristics.

Romance
You have a great deal of positive, fiery emotion that you express with great enthusiasm in your relationships. Your zest for love and sex is great, but you will see to it that both you and your partner also enjoy a lifestyle highlighted by as many enjoyable events as you can (or possibly cannot) afford. Be careful not to dominate your relationships too powerfully.

Your well-being
Everything that has been said about Leo health on pages 22 to 23 really does apply to you. Make sure that you take enough exercise to keep your system, and especially your spine and heart, in good working order.
Your liking for rich living could cause

The Moon in Leo

weight gain, so keep moving. This will also help to ensure that your circulation proves no problem. You no doubt love the sunshine and warm weather, and hate the cold. While you will probably tan well, remember to protect your skin with a powerful sun-screen cream or make-up.

Planning ahead

Because you like to do things in a refreshingly extravagant way, you will spend a lot of money, and so need to earn plenty of it. Let your financial motto be "large oaks from little acorns grow", and get pleasure from small

investments. Financial security is important to you, and although you tend to be extravagant you probably do not lack business sense.

Parenthood

Leo is the sign of parenthood and children, and you will make an excellent parent provided that you manage not to be too dogmatic in your attitude. Your interest, encouragement, and enthusiasm will help build a really good relationship between you. Keep abreast of your children's ideas and you will minimize the generation gap.

THE MOON IN
VIRGO

A CAUTIOUS, SOMEWHAT DAMNING INNER VOICE MAY SOMETIMES
CRITICIZE YOUR ACTIONS AND SAP YOUR SELF-CONFIDENCE.
YOUR INNER LEO SUN MUST COMBAT IT, SO THAT YOUR VIRGOAN
MOON WILL BE CONSTRUCTIVE AND HELPFUL.

Your earth sign Moon, while not particularly in harmony with your fire sign Sun, gives you a marvellously practical instinct that can stabilize the exuberance of your Leo Sun.

Self-expression

Your natural caution acts as a brake when you are tempted to show off or behave bumptiously. However, when confronted with a challenge, you sometimes feel a certain apprehension or lack of self-confidence. This is uncharacteristic for most Sun sign Leos, but it could happen in your case due to the influence of your Moon sign. If such a situation occurs, think of your achievements and allow yourself some pride.

You are very logical, with a powerful critical streak, and can cope better with detail than most Sun sign Leos. You will, however, have a tendency to immediately become involved with the minutiae of a project. Your Leo creativity may well find expression through gardening, or craftwork involving natural materials.

Romance

Your Virgoan Moon will cool your Leo emotions and add a refreshing modesty to your personality.

In spite of a passionate Leo nature, caution will be your keyword when developing a relationship. Anyone who is attracted to you will be critically dissected before you make a date, and certainly before they are allowed to deepen the relationship.

Your well-being

Virgo is a sign prone to worry and, more than many Sun sign Leos, you could suffer from this. Your approach should be a critical one: always assess your problems logically.

The Virgoan body area covers the stomach, and you may well have a bowel problem that tends to recur

The Moon in Virgo

when you are under stress. You will have a great deal of nervous energy and, should this result in tension, you may be prone to migraine. If this is the case, a relaxation technique such as yoga could be of help.

Planning ahead

Your Virgoan Moon will be a vital influence when it comes to finance. Leo extravagance is less likely to affect you than other Sun sign Leos. You could sometimes be better off than you realize; while you should not waste money, do not deny yourself things that make life enjoyable.

Parenthood

While all Sun sign Leos have fun with their children, be careful that you are not too critical of their efforts. It is a pity to see deflation and ebbing self-confidence at work. If you assess the younger generation's opinions and attitudes rationally, you will not suffer from generation gap problems.

THE MOON IN
LIBRA

WITH YOUR MOON IN LIBRA, YOU MAY ASSUME LAZINESS AND
GIVE THE IMPRESSION OF BEING LAID BACK, BUT A
LEO SUN NEEDS TO LIVE EVERY DAY TO THE FULL. YOUR
MOON WILL ALSO HELP YOU TO ENJOY LIFE.

The combination of the fire element of your Sun and the air element of your Moon adds some interesting aspects to your personality.

Self-expression
You will respond to challenges with typical Leo enthusiasm. Your Libran Moon will ensure that this enthusiasm will be governed and controlled in a calm, relaxed, and diplomatic way.

With indecisiveness being the worst Libran fault, you may have uncharacteristic second thoughts, especially when under pressure or in a stressful situation. At such times, make use of your Leo organizational ability. It will enable you to control your thinking processes.

Both Leos and Librans love the good life, comfort, and luxury. In this area you will experience no conflict between your Sun and Moon signs; you have the ability to sit back, relax, and simply enjoy being sociable.

Romance
You make a wonderful lover, and are, no doubt, very considerate of your partner's needs. In some respects you may not feel psychologically whole until you are settled in a permanent relationship. Be careful: in your desire to relate in depth, you may have a tendency to commit yourself prematurely. At times you could expect rather too much of a partner, simply because you, yourself, have so much to give.

Your well-being
The Libran body area covers the kidneys and the lumbar region of the back. As Leo rules the spine and back you may well be subject to pain in that area. The quality of the mattress you sleep on is important. You may also tend to get rather a lot of headaches, which could be due to a slight kidney upset. Seek medical advice whenever necessary.

The Moon in Libra

Good food is another luxury enjoyed by both Leo and Libra; Librans tend to put on weight more easily, since many have a somewhat slow metabolism. If you have a tendency to move in a languid way, and walk slowly, try to speed up your metabolism through exercise.

Planning ahead

Leo extravagance and love of quality will certainly eat into your finances. Since you may be bored by bookkeeping and investing, you would be wise to seek sound financial advice from an expert, and to start a regular savings scheme.

Parenthood

Do not allow Libran indecisiveness to undermine your positive Leo qualities in your role as a parent. Your Leo Sun sign will ensure that you enjoy parenthood, and your enthusiasm for your children's interests will spur them on to greater effort. Keep aware of their concerns and opinions, in order to avoid the generation gap.

THE MOON IN
SCORPIO

LEO QUALITIES ARE GIVEN DEPTH, INTENSITY, AND A POWERFUL,
EMOTIONALLY ORIENTATED DRIVING FORCE BY A SCORPIO
MOON. YOU MUST BE EMOTIONALLY INVOLVED IN YOUR WORK,
AND ENJOY A FULFILLING RELATIONSHIP.

You are likely to have very strong resources of both physical and emotional energy and, for the sake of your inner fulfilment, it is vital that your lifestyle is rewarding enough to allow them full rein.

Self-expression
You must be psychologically involved in your work. If this is not the case, you will feel discontented, and brooding dissatisfaction will get the better of you.

Both Leo and Scorpio are of the fixed quality, so you may well have to consciously develop the art of being flexible. Try to keep an open mind, and take heed if someone accuses you of being dogmatic or stubborn. Be firm, but not intractable.

Romance
Possessing both the fiery emotion of Leo and the deep, intense emotion of Scorpio, you will express your feelings very passionately indeed. You will be among the most passionate of lovers and will have a great need for a responsible partner who is as highly sexed as yourself. The worst Scorpio fault is jealousy, which is not something that is usually felt by Sun sign Leos. Should you succumb to it, try to be rational and to allow Leo magnanimity full expression.

Your well-being
The Scorpio body area covers the genitals. Regular well-woman tests are advisable, and men should examine their testicles regularly, as good preventive measures.

While some people with a Scorpio emphasis are lean and wiry, others tend to be stocky. If you fall into the latter category you may have a slightly slow metabolism. Try to speed it up through exercise. Both Leo and Scorpio like to live life to the full, and enjoy quality food and wines. These

The Moon in Scorpio

can, of course, adversely affect your body shape. If you need to lose weight, gradually readjust your general food intake, and develop a more sensibly balanced diet.

Planning ahead

You have excellent business instincts. When investing, you will probably do well to follow them. Your Leo and Scorpio fondness for quality and beautiful things is likely to cost you a great deal of money. Therefore a

great amount of your motivation should be geared to making as much money as possible.

Parenthood

It is possible that you may be a strict parent. While you will like being with your children, you may be a little too demanding. If you are not too dogmatic, you will share a good relationship. As your children grow up, they will develop different opinions to yours. Try to accept them.

THE MOON IN
SAGITTARIUS

YOUR SUN AND MOON SIGNS OFFER A LIVELY COMBINATION, WITH
THE SAGITTARIAN MOON ADDING A CASUAL STREAK
TO THE LEO SUN. YOU NEED ADVENTURE IN STUDY AND TRAVEL,
AND YOU WILL COPE WITH DAUNTING CHALLENGES.

Provided that you are consciously aware of one or two negative tendencies, you should be able to make your Leo Sun and Sagittarian Moon work together for you.

Self-expression
You have a marvellously positive enthusiasm that surfaces as soon as you are challenged in any way, or when someone makes a suggestion that pleases you. You will at once want to encourage them, and as long as you keep your enthusiasm burning brightly you will ensure that, together, you can achieve whatever the objective may be. You have a great capacity for immediately grasping the overall picture of any situation, but should accept the fact that you are easily bored by detail.

You are very versatile, and to satisfy this area of your personality you should have a variety of physical, mental, and creative interests.

Your emotions are powerful, and it is good for you to involve yourself in a cause about which you feel strongly.

Romance
It is in the area of love and relationships that your powerful feelings can be most fully expressed. You may fall in love very quickly – perhaps even at first sight – and your love of life, enthusiasm for love and sex, and warm, affectionate nature will soon break down your prospective partner's defences. Although you are eager for a permanent relationship, you also have a greater need for freedom of expression than most Sun sign Leos.

Your well-being
The Sagittarian body area covers the hips and thighs, where most women of this sign tend to put on weight. It is advisable for you to try to keep to a fairly light diet. The Sagittarian organ

The Moon in Sagittarius

is the liver; as a result you may tend to suffer rather more from hangovers than most Leos.

Planning ahead

You may well have a sneaking liking for financial risk-taking, or even a gambling instinct. Your Leo Sun gives you extravagant tastes, so be careful. Do not risk any more money than you can afford to lose, and do not be tempted by get-rich-quick schemes. You could, all too easily, lose a great deal of money, so always be prepared to take sound professional advice in this area.

Parenthood

Although most Leos enjoy parenthood, some tend to be rather formal in their relationships with their children. This is less likely in your case, and you will not find it difficult to enjoy their enthusiasms.

Similarly, while you will not want your children to be clones of yourself, they should not, on the whole, be bored by your own varied interests. Try to develop any creative talent that they inherit. You will be able to keep abreast of their opinions, and should suffer very few problems with the generation gap.

THE MOON IN
CAPRICORN

YOU WILL BE AMBITIOUS, AND WILL SUCCEED IN WHATEVER YOU
PUT YOUR MIND TO. ALLOW YOUR EARTH SIGN MOON TO
TELL YOU INSTINCTIVELY WHEN TO MAKE IMPORTANT MOVES,
BUT DO NOT LET IT COOL YOUR WARM LEO SUN.

Your Capricornian Moon endows you with qualities that contrast strongly with those of your Leo Sun, but you should be able to blend them and make them work for you.

Self-expression
Caution and a serious, well-considered response to most situations are characteristic of you, and your Leo enthusiasm will be controlled by a practical and cool approach to important issues. But your Leo love of life will always shine through, and it is extremely likely that you have an instinctive, dry sense of humour that is more amusing than you think.

Your Capricornian Moon may have a slight dampening effect on the warmth of your Leo Sun, making you feel somewhat gloomy and depressed at times. Clouds may darken your psychological landscape, until the influence of your Leo Sun takes over.

Leos are generally very ambitious, and like to have their own tiny kingdoms to rule. Capricornians can also be extremely ambitious, and are always aspiring to rise to greater things. If all goes well, this combined attitude will help you achieve whatever you set your heart on.

Romance
Your Capricornian Moon will make you rather cautious in your attitude and approach to the opposite sex. Once committed, both Leos and Capricornians are usually faithful. But you may not be averse to a little social climbing, and should curb any tendency to show off.

Your well-being
The Capricornian body area covers the knees and shins. If you suffer from stiffness of the joints, exercise may help. The teeth are also Capricorn-ruled, so make sure you

The Moon in Capricorn

have regular dental check-ups. Your skin may tan less easily than that of most Leos, so wear a good sun screen.

Planning ahead

While your Leo Sun urges you to spend and enjoy your money, your Capricornian instincts will encourage you to take a practical line and make you a clever investor. You probably have good business sense, and should do well if you start your own business. For you the most important thing is to enjoy your money. Do not waste time

and energy spending it simply to impress other people. Spend it, instead, on your loved ones. Your Moon will work for you and prevent you from spending unwisely.

Parenthood

If your children ever accuse you of being pompous or a fuddy-duddy, be careful to take note. Avoid being so involved with making money for them, and trying to provide everything they need, that you miss out on really knowing them.

THE MOON IN
AQUARIUS

LEO AND AQUARIUS ARE POLAR OR OPPOSITE ZODIAC SIGNS, SO YOU
WERE BORN UNDER A FULL MOON. YOU COULD SUFFER FROM
PERIODS OF RESTLESSNESS, AND MUST AVOID STUBBORNNESS. LET
AQUARIAN ORIGINALITY IGNITE LEONINE CREATIVITY.

Each of us, in one way or another, expresses elements of our polar or opposite sign, the sign that lies across the Zodiac from our Sun sign. For Leo, the polar sign is Aquarius, and as the Moon was in that sign when you were born, the polarity is emphasized in a most striking way.

Self-expression

You have a very independent streak, and like to do things in a way that is just right for you. It may be that you have evolved a unique lifestyle that you guard jealously.

You will express your originality in a variety of ways. Perhaps you like to look a little different, or maybe your job is an unusual one. Even more conducive for your inner fulfilment, your Leo creativity could be spiced with originality.

It is important for you develop flexibility, since both Leo and Aquarius are of the fixed quality,

which tends to make you stubborn. Always aim to complete projects, or you will feel dissatisfied and restless. This is one effect of being born at the time of the Full Moon.

Romance

You may tend to distance yourself from prospective partners, feeling that you are not yet ready for total commitment. However, anyone with an Aquarian influence is also very romantic and, once a partner has broken the ice with you, you are capable of very faithful love, and a rewarding sex life – if you are given enough room to breathe, and allowed some independence.

Your well-being

The Aquarian body area covers the ankles, and you may easily twist yours. The circulation is also Aquarius-ruled and, as this is so strongly related to the heart, the Leo

The Moon in Aquarius

organ, you should make sure that your blood flows really freely. You probably like cold, crisp weather more than most Leos, and may enjoy participating in winter sports.

Planning ahead

You could well be attracted to very glitzy things, for example unusual mirrors, vases, and of course jewellery. These can prove expensive and not terribly durable. As a result, your finances may suffer. Try to develop a practical attitude towards money, and take professional advice when you have any cash to invest.

Parenthood

You will be a lively parent, but your unpredictability may leave your children uncertain where they stand with you. You are forward-looking, and could want to bring them up in an unusual way. This can work well, but some children feel more secure with a strict set of rules to live by.

THE MOON IN
PISCES

YOUR HIGHLY EMOTIONAL LEO FIRE SIGN IS SENSITIZED BY THE
EMOTION OF YOUR WATER SIGN PISCEAN MOON. IF YOU ARE
DISCIPLINED, AND CHANNEL YOUR SUPERB RESOURCES, YOU WILL
ACHIEVE MUCH – ESPECIALLY IN CREATIVE OR CARING WORK.

While your Sun and Moon signs suggest very different qualities, there is also great sympathy between them, which is emphasized by emotion and creative potential.

Self-expression

At times you could feel pretty unsure of yourself. It is very important for you to realize that you could deceive yourself. Do not doubt yourself, or resort to putting yourself down. Allow your Piscean Moon to be a source of inspiration and imagination; channel its force creatively. However you do this, express your abundant potential with all the Leo confidence in the world. Be bold, and you will achieve inner fulfilment.

Romance

You have a very powerful emotional energy that you may, to an extent, express towards humanitarian causes and in the relief of suffering, but it

will mostly be directed towards your partner. You are capable of a really grand passion, reaching heights of happiness and the depths of despair.

There is a great dramatic sense in your attitude to your lover – this is present in most Sun sign Leos, and in your case is made even more colourful by your Piscean Moon. You will be very sensitive to your partners' needs, and will probably put them on a pedestal. Learn to be forthcoming: you know what gives you pleasure, and should not hold back.

Your well-being

The Piscean body area covers the feet. Do not hesitate to spend money on visits to the chiropodist if you have problems with your feet.

It can be difficult for those with a Piscean influence to be disciplined. When it comes to exercise and regular meals you may, for instance, simply not bother if you are alone. Try to get

The Moon in Pisces

into and stick to a regular routine; the Leo in you really needs it, if you are to express your potential consistently and to the full. Any exercise that inspires you will do you all-round good, to both body and soul, and by exercising you will overcome a Piscean vulnerability to flabbiness.

Planning ahead

Being both very generous and something of a soft touch, you are probably less good with money than many Leos. Remember, however, that some people will take advantage of you, so be firm if they ask for a loan. While you should seek financial advice before investing, you may wish to put money into building a specific collection of some kind. This will be fun and, if properly managed, a good investment in itself.

Parenthood

You will be a sympathetic, enthusiastic, and encouraging parent, but do not allow your sensitive reactions to your children's needs and suggestions to get the better of you. Keep in tune with their ideas and concerns, and you will be able to bridge the generation gap.

MOON CHARTS

REFER TO THE FOLLOWING TABLES TO DISCOVER YOUR MOON SIGN.
THE PRECEDING PAGES WILL TELL YOU ABOUT ITS QUALITIES.

By referring to the Moon charts opposite and overleaf, look up the year of your birth and the Zodiacal glyph for your birth month. Refer next to the Moon Table (*below, left*) in which the days of the month are listed against a number. The number against the day of the month in which you were born indicates how many Zodiacal glyphs (*below, right*) must be counted before you reach your Moon sign. You may have to count to Pisces and return to Aries. For example, given the birthdate 21 May 1991, you initially need to find the Moon sign

for the first day of May in that year. It is Sagittarius (♐). With the birthdate falling on the 21st, nine signs must be added. The Moon sign for this birth date is therefore Virgo (♍).

Note that because the Moon moves so quickly, it is beyond the scope of this little book to provide a detailed chart of its positions. For more detailed horoscopes, consult an astrologer, but if you feel that this chart gives a result that does not seem to apply to you, read the pages for the signs either before or after the one indicated; one of the three will apply.

MOON TABLE

DAYS OF THE MONTH AND NUMBER OF
SIGNS THAT SHOULD BE ADDED

DAY	ADD	DAY	ADD	DAY	ADD	DAY	ADD
1	0	9	4	17	7	25	11
2	1	10	4	18	8	26	11
3	1	11	5	19	8	27	12
4	1	12	5	20	9	28	12
5	2	13	5	21	9	29	1
6	2	14	6	22	10	30	1
7	3	15	6	23	10	31	2
8	3	16	7	24	10		

ZODIACAL GLYPHS

♈	Aries
♉	Taurus
♊	Gemini
♋	Cancer
♌	Leo
♍	Virgo
♎	Libra
♏	Scorpio
♐	Sagittarius
♑	Capricorn
♒	Aquarius
♓	Pisces

	1923	1924	1925	1926	1927	1928	1929	1930	1931	1932	1933	1934	1935
JAN	♊	♏	♈	♌	♐	♈	♍	♑	♉	♎	♓	♋	♏
FEB	♌	♐	♉	♍	♑	♊	♏	♓	♋	♐	♈	♌	♑
MAR	♌	♑	♉	♍	♒	♋	♏	♓	♋	♐	♉	♍	♑
APR	♎	♓	♋	♏	♈	♍	♑	♉	♍	♒	♊	♎	♓
MAY	♏	♈	♌	♐	♉	♎	♒	♊	♎	♓	♋	♐	♈
JUN	♑	♉	♍	♒	♋	♏	♓	♌	♐	♉	♍	♑	♊
JUL	♒	♋	♍	♓	♌	♐	♈	♍	♑	♊	♎	♓	♋
AUG	♈	♌	♐	♉	♍	♒	♊	♏	♓	♋	♐	♈	♌
SEP	♉	♎	♒	♋	♏	♓	♌	♐	♈	♍	♑	♊	♎
OCT	♊	♏	♓	♌	♐	♉	♍	♑	♉	♎	♓	♋	♏
NOV	♌	♑	♉	♍	♑	♊	♏	♓	♋	♐	♈	♌	♑
DEC	♍	♒	♊	♎	♓	♌	♐	♈	♌	♑	♉	♍	♒

	1936	1937	1938	1939	1940	1941	1942	1943	1944	1945	1946	1947	1948
JAN	♈	♌	♑	♉	♍	♒	♊	♎	♓	♌	♐	♈	♍
FEB	♉	♎	♒	♊	♏	♈	♌	♐	♉	♍	♑	♊	♎
MAR	♊	♎	♒	♋	♐	♈	♌	♐	♉	♎	♒	♊	♏
APR	♌	♐	♈	♌	♑	♉	♎	♒	♋	♏	♓	♌	♑
MAY	♍	♑	♉	♎	♒	♊	♏	♓	♌	♐	♉	♍	♒
JUN	♎	♒	♋	♏	♈	♌	♐	♉	♎	♒	♊	♏	♓
JUL	♏	♈	♌	♑	♉	♍	♒	♊	♏	♌	♐	♈	♈
AUG	♑	♉	♎	♒	♋	♏	♈	♌	♐	♉	♍	♑	♊
SEP	♓	♋	♏	♈	♌	♑	♉	♍	♒	♋	♏	♓	♌
OCT	♈	♌	♑	♉	♎	♒	♊	♎	♓	♌	♐	♈	♍
NOV	♊	♎	♒	♊	♏	♈	♌	♐	♉	♍	♑	♊	♏
DEC	♋	♏	♓	♌	♑	♉	♍	♑	♊	♎	♒	♋	♐

	1949	1950	1951	1952	1953	1954	1955	1956	1957	1958	1959	1960	1961
JAN	♑	♊	♎	♓	♋	♏	♈	♌	♑	♉	♍	♒	♋
FEB	♓	♋	♐	♈	♍	♑	♉	♎	♒	♊	♏	♈	♌
MAR	♓	♋	♐	♉	♍	♑	♊	♏	♓	♋	♏	♈	♌
APR	♉	♍	♒	♊	♎	♓	♋	♐	♈	♌	♑	♊	♎
MAY	♊	♎	♓	♋	♐	♈	♍	♑	♉	♎	♒	♋	♏
JUN	♌	♐	♈	♍	♑	♊	♎	♓	♋	♐	♈	♌	♑
JUL	♍	♑	♊	♎	♓	♋	♏	♈	♌	♑	♉	♍	♒
AUG	♏	♓	♋	♐	♈	♍	♑	♉	♎	♒	♊	♏	♈
SEP	♐	♈	♍	♑	♊	♎	♒	♋	♐	♈	♌	♑	♊
OCT	♑	♊	♎	♓	♋	♏	♓	♌	♑	♉	♍	♒	♋
NOV	♓	♋	♏	♈	♍	♑	♉	♎	♒	♊	♏	♈	♌
DEC	♈	♌	♑	♊	♎	♒	♊	♏	♓	♌	♐	♉	♍

	1962	1963	1964	1965	1966	1967	1968	1969	1970	1971	1972	1973	1974
JAN	♏	♓	♌	♐	♈	♍	♑	♊	♎	♒	♋	♐	♈
FEB	♐	♉	♍	♒	♊	♏	♓	♋	♏	♈	♍	♑	♉
MAR	♐	♉	♎	♒	♊	♏	♈	♌	♐	♉	♍	♑	♊
APR	♒	♋	♏	♈	♌	♑	♉	♍	♒	♊	♏	♓	♋
MAY	♓	♌	♐	♉	♍	♒	♊	♎	♓	♋	♐	♈	♍
JUN	♉	♎	♒	♊	♏	♓	♌	♐	♉	♍	♑	♊	♎
JUL	♊	♏	♓	♌	♐	♈	♍	♑	♊	♎	♓	♋	♐
AUG	♌	♐	♉	♎	♒	♊	♏	♓	♋	♏	♈	♍	♑
SEP	♍	♒	♋	♏	♓	♋	♐	♉	♍	♑	♊	♎	♓
OCT	♏	♓	♌	♐	♈	♍	♒	♊	♎	♒	♋	♐	♈
NOV	♐	♉	♎	♒	♊	♎	♓	♋	♐	♈	♍	♑	♉
DEC	♑	♊	♏	♓	♋	♐	♈	♌	♑	♉	♎	♒	♊

	1975	1976	1977	1978	1979	1980	1981	1982	1983	1984	1985	1986	1987
JAN	♌	♑	♉	♍	♒	♊	♏	♓	♌	♐	♉	♍	♑
FEB	♎	♒	♋	♏	♈	♌	♐	♉	♍	♒	♊	♎	♓
MAR	♎	♓	♋	♏	♈	♍	♑	♉	♎	♒	♊	♏	♓
APR	♐	♈	♍	♑	♊	♎	♒	♋	♏	♈	♌	♑	♉
MAY	♑	♉	♎	♒	♋	♏	♓	♌	♐	♉	♍	♒	♊
JUN	♓	♋	♐	♈	♌	♑	♉	♎	♒	♊	♏	♓	♌
JUL	♈	♌	♑	♏	♍	♒	♋	♏	♓	♌	♐	♉	♍
AUG	♉	♎	♓	♋	♏	♈	♌	♐	♈	♎	♒	♊	♎
SEP	♋	♐	♈	♌	♐	♊	♎	♒	♊	♏	♓	♌	♐
OCT	♌	♑	♉	♍	♒	♋	♏	♓	♋	♐	♉	♍	♑
NOV	♎	♓	♋	♏	♓	♌	♐	♉	♍	♒	♊	♎	♓
DEC	♏	♈	♌	♐	♉	♍	♑	♊	♎	♓	♋	♐	♈

	1988	1989	1990	1991	1992	1993	1994	1995	1996	1997	1998	1999	2000
JAN	♊	♎	♒	♋	♏	♈	♌	♑	♉	♎	♒	♊	♏
FEB	♋	♐	♈	♍	♑	♉	♎	♒	♋	♏	♈	♌	♐
MAR	♌	♐	♉	♍	♒	♊	♎	♓	♋	♏	♈	♌	♑
APR	♍	♒	♊	♏	♓	♋	♐	♈	♍	♑	♊	♎	♓
MAY	♏	♓	♌	♐	♈	♍	♑	♉	♎	♒	♋	♏	♈
JUN	♐	♉	♍	♑	♊	♎	♓	♋	♐	♈	♌	♑	♉
JUL	♑	♊	♎	♒	♋	♐	♈	♌	♑	♉	♎	♒	♋
AUG	♓	♌	♐	♈	♍	♑	♉	♎	♓	♋	♏	♓	♌
SEP	♉	♍	♑	♊	♏	♓	♋	♏	♈	♌	♑	♉	♎
OCT	♊	♎	♒	♋	♐	♈	♌	♑	♉	♎	♒	♊	♏
NOV	♌	♐	♈	♍	♑	♉	♎	♒	♋	♏	♈	♌	♑
DEC	♍	♑	♉	♎	♒	♋	♏	♈	♌	♐	♉	♍	♒

THE SOLAR SYSTEM

THE STARS, OTHER THAN THE SUN, PLAY NO PART IN THE SCIENCE
OF ASTROLOGY. ASTROLOGERS USE ONLY THE BODIES IN THE
SOLAR SYSTEM, EXCLUDING THE EARTH, TO CALCULATE HOW OUR
LIVES AND PERSONALITIES CHANGE.

Pluto
Pluto takes 246 years to travel around
the Sun. It affects our unconscious
instincts and urges, gives us strength
in difficulty, and perhaps emphasizes
any inherent cruel streak.

Neptune
Neptune stays in each sign for 14
years. At best it makes us sensitive
and imaginative; at worst it
encourages deceit and carelessness,
making us worry.

Uranus
Uranus's influence can make us
friendly, kind, eccentric, inventive,
and unpredictable.

Saturn
In ancient times, Saturn was the most
distant known planet. Its influence
can limit our ambition and make us
either overly cautious (but practical),
or reliable and self-disciplined.

PLUTO

NEPTUNE

URANUS

SATURN

Jupiter

Jupiter encourages expansion, optimism, generosity, and breadth of vision. It can, however, also make us wasteful, extravagant, and conceited.

Mars

Much associated with energy, anger, violence, selfishness, and a strong sex drive, Mars also encourages decisiveness and leadership.

JUPITER

MARS

Earth

Every planet contributes to the environment of the Solar System, and a person born on Venus would no doubt be influenced by our own planet in some way.

The Moon

Although it is a satellite of the Earth, the Moon is known in astrology as a planet. It lies about 240,000 miles from the Earth and, astrologically, is second in importance to the Sun.

MERCURY

THE MOON

VENUS

EARTH

The Sun

The Sun, the only star used by astrologers, influences the way we present ourselves to the world – our image or personality; the "us" we show to other people.

Venus

The planet of love and partnership, Venus can emphasize all our best personal qualities. It may also encourage us to be lazy, impractical, and too dependent on other people.

Mercury

The planet closest to the Sun affects our intellect. It can make us inquisitive, versatile, argumentative, perceptive, and clever, but maybe also inconsistent, cynical, and sarcastic.